On My Way

By, Clarence Gilles

ACKNOWLEDGEMENTS

On My Way, is dedicated to my wife, Vi, who spent endless hours reading and critiquing this book with me. I also dedicate the book to a special friend whose desire to find Christ led to the inspiration of this book. His sharing of the circles illustration with others and his continual persistence in asking me to write the book provided the encouragement needed to bring it to fruition. It was his question, "How can I get to know Christ better?", that the Holy Spirit used to inspire the idea of the circles. It also led me to take a deeper look at my own continuous and progressive conversion. The book once written may never have been published if God had not sent Tim Ireland into my life to assist me in formatting the book so that it could be published.

No part of this book may be reproduced in any form by any means, electronic, mechanical, recorded, photocopied or otherwise without prior express permission in written form from the copyright owner.

A DBA of On-Demand Publishing LLC, part of the Amazon group of companies.

Copyright © by Clarence Gilles 2014.

All rights reserved.

CONTENTS

Foreword 1

Introduction 4

Chapter I -- How the Circles Concept Came To Be 8

Chapter II -- Explanation of Each Circle 15

Chapter III -- Outside of the Circles 17

Chapter IV -- Inside the Orange Circle 25

Chapter V -- Inside the Dark Blue Circle 34

Chapter VI -- Inside the Light Blue Circle 42

Chapter VII -- Inside the Lavender Circle 51

Chapter VIII -- Inside the Gold Circle 65

Chapter IX -- Inside the Red Circle 79

Our Continuous Conversion 87

Conclusion 90

REFERENCES:

THE HOLY BIBLE, NEW INTERNATIONAL VERSION®, NIV® Copyright © 1973, 1978, 1984, 2011 by Biblica, Inc.® Used by permission. All rights reserved worldwide.

The Word Among Us, August 2013.

Excerpts from Cardinal Ratzinger's year of faith address, "The Easter Miracle", Pentecost 1998.

Church of the Incarnation Centerville, Ohio, church bulletin November 18, 2012.

Excerpts from Auxiliary Bishop Joseph Binzer, Catholic Telegraph Jan. 2015.

Foreword

We are all on our way but in a different place on our walk with Christ. Our backgrounds, experiences and preferences all have an impact on where we place Christ in our life. This book, *On My Way,* is for anyone who desires to grow closer to Christ. It's simple format makes it easy to determine your own path to salvation. As you ponder each circle, you will recognize where you are and determine how to get from where you are today to where you want to be for eternity. No matter where you are in your spiritual walk, you are represented in this book. You can grow in your faith if you have a desire to grow, and you can help others grow in their faith by sharing yours. The book is primarily a book for self-reflection, but can be shared with others in a group study.

The journey never ends and God's time is not our time, so be patient in reading the book. Listen to the Holy Spirit as you read it. The book in itself can give a clearer understanding of how to proceed on your journey.

There are a variety of programs, activities and exercises mentioned in the text. The benefit derived from them will depend upon your desire to become Christ centered. If you start with an open mind and heart, you will discover where God wants you to be and how to get there.

While I am Catholic, the circles represent various phases of spiritual growth that Christians go through as they progress in their relationship with Christ. The goal is to come to the point where everything we do is for the love of God, not self, as we live this life in preparation for eternity.

The Bible verses come from THE HOLY BIBLE, NEW INTERNATIONAL VERSION®, NIV® Whether you are Protestant or Catholic, the same Bible verses, insights and challenges remain.

The first step in any journey is taking the initiative to move toward your destination. The first step in reading On My Way is to start at the beginning even though you may feel you are well on your way to your destination. The second step is to determine where you presently are on the path. As you go through this book and reflect on the circles, you will see yourself, family members and friends.

Everyone is represented within the circles illustration. When you finish this study, you will discover through prayer, scripture and self-reflection, your personal road map for a closer relationship with Christ. You may also discover how you can help family and friends proceed on their journey.

This is your own personal journey to a closer relationship with Christ. Open your mind and heart to allow God to speak to you as the Holy Spirit will be your guide.

The most benefit will come from reflection on the questions at the end of each chapter. You can be completely honest with yourself because God already knows you and where He wants to lead you.

After each chapter a page is provided for you to write down thoughts that came to mind in reading the chapter. One purpose of the book is to encourage you to share your journey with others. Writing down what came to mind then becomes your travel log,

The book can provide a great opportunity for a small group study. Answering the questions along with and jotting down thoughts and experiences can help facilitate spiritual growth.

Introduction

As for my walk with Christ, I was a cradle Catholic attending weekly Mass and praying before meals. I had a few statues that I purchased while attending St. Anthony Grade School which I prominently displayed in my room. I put them away when I entered high school. When I was growing up our family had a family Bible, but I can't remember anyone ever reading it.

My faith life changed when I met my future wife, who was a devout Catholic. After we married, we still did not read the Bible at home. We did, however, read the children's Bible and other books about the saints to our children, and they attended parochial schools.

For 17 years we fulfilled Catholic expectations of going to Mass and supporting the church. That all changed for us after our three day Cum Christo (Cursillo) weekends. I was 41 years of age. On the weekend we discovered how much God loves us. It created a desire within us to study God's word. We started not only reading the Bible, but attending Bible study groups with a desire to learn more about our Lord and develop a closer relationship with Him. We came to realize that if we were seriously interested in getting to know Christ, we needed to study His word. It is always amazing to me how succinct scripture is and yet it provides endless insights.

Jeff Cavins, creator of *The Great Adventure* and other Bible studies says, "If we read the Bible carefully, we will see that Jesus is raising us to a new level of holiness and empowering us to live it."

Hopefully, reading the chosen Bible verses for each circle will provide insight and clarification for the spiritual significance of each circle. I am confident that the idea of the circles came as a gift of the Spirit when I sought His help. May the circles also guide you on your personal path to holiness?

The circles are your tools for self-reflection. Mentally reflect upon your journey up to the present time. Upon finishing the book, re-evaluate the circles and where you desire to be. Finally, make plans for your future growth, employing the various thoughts and ideas that came to mind while reading the book. With the Spirit's guidance you will discern the best way to get from your present place to where you wish to be.

Today is the day and now is the time for all people who declare they are Christians to re-examine their lives. Are we truly doing what Christ has asked of us in scripture? It is especially fitting for Catholics since Pope Benedict declared the "Year of Faith" in 2012, asking the church to become more vibrant in living the faith. And who is the church? We are the church, all of us who believe in Christ as the Savior who offers us eternal life. Let us open our hearts and minds to accept what the Spirit imparts and pray that He gives us the courage to proceed on our walk towards Christ.

I hope the circles encourage you to seek ways to grow in faith, to recognize the opportunities the Lord presents for growth and to accept the challenge of living a Christ centered life. When you focus on Christ, others will take notice, and in the process you will encourage friends, family, acquaintances and those you meet to consider where they are on their path to Christ.

Preparation

Before beginning each chapter, I encourage you to take some time to recognize that Christ is with you at this very moment. In a quiet setting ask the Holy Spirit to reside within you. Open up your inner self to allow the Spirit to enter so that you can feel his promptings.

Take a moment to say this prayer to the Holy Spirit:

> Come Holy Spirit, fill the hearts of your faithful and enkindle in us the fire of your love. Send forth your Spirit, and we shall be created, and You shall renew the face of the earth.
>
> Oh God, who by the light of the Holy Spirit, did instruct the hearts of the faithful, grant that by the same Holy Spirit we may be truly wise and ever rejoice in His consolation through Christ Our Lord. Amen.

There are questions after each chapter to induce thought and recollection about your spiritual life and personal journey.

One page after each chapter is provided for you to write down thoughts that came to mind in reading the chapter. Writing down what came to mind becomes your travel log

Chapter I -- How the Circles Concept Came To Be

In November 2008, I stayed with a friend as I often did when visiting Milwaukee. On this occasion he wanted to know what I was doing with all my new found time in retirement. I told him I had just finished writing a talk on "Ideals" for Cursillo. He asked me what Cursillo was and what my talk was all about. He starting asking questions about the talk and after several questions I said, "Why don't I just send the talk to you?"

A few weeks later, after he read the talk, he asked me to send him a prayer. I sent him the Thomas Merton prayer (below), thinking he was looking for guidance.

> MY LORD GOD, I have no idea where I am going. I do not see the road ahead of me. I cannot know for certain where it will end. Nor do I really know myself, and the fact that I think that I am following Your will does not mean that I am actually doing so. But I believe that the desire to please You does in fact please You. And I hope I have that desire in all that I am doing.
>
> I hope that I will never do anything apart from that desire. And I know that if I do this, You will lead me by the right road, though I may know nothing about it. Therefore I will trust You always though I may seem to be lost and in the shadow of death. I will not fear, for

You are ever with me, and You will never leave me to face my perils alone.

Two weeks later he called back, saying. "It isn't working." "What's not working?" I asked. "The prayer", he said. I mentioned that maybe what he wanted was not what God had in mind. I told him I would send him the prayer to the Holy Spirit for guidance, which you read in the introduction. After this discussion, we talked about my coming to Milwaukee, Wisconsin to tour his plant. Now that I was retired, he thought I might be interested in promoting his company's products in Ohio.

In January of 2009, I made the trip to Milwaukee. After touring the plant, we went to the conference room where he gave me a list of some distributors to review while he took care of other business. When he returned, instead of asking me about the distributors, he asked, "How can I get to know Christ better?" Now I understood why the Lord called me there.

I was a bit surprised by his question, "How can I get to know Christ better?" I told him I needed some time to think about it. He stepped out for a few minutes to give me time to think about an answer. I implored the Holy Spirit for some help. I started to think about the progression of my faith life and that of others I knew over the years. How did their faith life start and progress over time? I thought about the different steps we would need to go through to finally be one with Christ. Then I started drawing the circles and wrote inside each one what it represented.

When I showed it to my friend, he commented that it looked complicated, so I redrew it putting the descriptions above, below and inside the circles. My writing was not very legible, and the circles did not look like circles at all. Nevertheless he took my drawing, saying he could read it.

A few days later my friend called and said he had shown the circles to people at his church. They were enthusiastic about its simplicity and felt the diagram was a helpful tool to identify where they were in their faith life. I was encouraged that my friend was interested enough in the circles to show and discuss them with others. The positive response inspired me to continue to develop the concept and provide supporting documentation.

With the help of the Spirit, my friend was able to see where he was on his journey to know Christ. The circles provided a simple illustration to address a complex subject. They represent all of our lives. Where we are and end up is a matter of our personal desire, our will and how it conforms to God's will. The circles provide direction for a path to holiness, which through the grace of God, prayer and commitment; can be attained by any one of us.

Moving through the circles is a long process because we have to look closely at ourselves, who we are and what we believe. It takes determination, but with the Holy Spirit as our guide and the Father as our strength, we can succeed.

I told my friend that I was in the **Dark Blue** circle for 26 years. He said, "It won't take me that long to move into the next circle."

I replied, "You have not been convicted yet." He said, "What is conviction?" I said, "It is the revealing of our hidden nature or sin that we do not see. As one gets closer to Christ, it is brought to light through the Spirit. Others may have seen it, but we do not see it in ourselves."

My main struggle is with pride which I find difficult to overcome because it is a part of me. I now recognize it, as it pops up frequently and I continue to work to overcome it with the grace of God as He provides the gift of humility. Conviction in this sense should not be confused with a strong belief in something.

Everyone fits into one of these circles, but we do not just cross from one circle into another. We often gravitate, as a hue in the color of a rainbow. There are variations as we move from one to the other.

People may often vacillate between the circles because of career moves, changes in circumstances, people we meet, or God's intervention. Many times people lose even what faith they once had if their progressive conversion is not continually nurtured.

Since the journey is personal, you cannot impose your journey upon someone else nor push others where they do not want to go. The desire must come from within and from the Spirit. All that any of us can do is be open to opportunities to grow spiritually and to offer encouragement to others as they pursue their journey with Christ.

The way we live our lives can be an example for others. In addition we can plant seeds for the Spirit to water. (We will talk about planting seeds later.) We also have the power of prayer. We know that when we open our hearts to God and put our trust in Him, he answers our prayers.

Take time to study two statements that summarize why we need to continue putting effort into growing spiritually and seeking a closer relationship with Christ. Put some thought into them, especially the second statement. The statements are from the *Word Among Us*.

> Christ is the bridge between us here on earth and God the Father in heaven.

> Apart from Christ we will never know God, the meaning of life, the result of death or the purpose for which we were made. [1]

What do you think about the above statements?

_____

---

[1] *The Word Among Us,* August 2013 Issue

Questions for self-reflection or group discussion:

How would you answer, the question? "How can I get to know Christ better?"

_____

_____

_____

_____

Do you have a desire to grow spiritually?

_____

_____

_____

Chapter 1 is the first leg of your journey. I encourage you to write down what your thoughts have been up to this point on the next page.

What are your thoughts as you start this journey?

Chapter II -- Explanation of Each Circle

Where are you now? Where do you want to be?

Outside of the circles: UNAWARE OF OR REJECT GOD. Lack knowledge of God, are actively defiant towards God or reject Christ. Focus may be on money, fame, prestige, power, family, sports, recreation etc. (Hebrews 12:6-7) (Mathew 9: 1-7) (Mark 2:1-11) (James 5: 13-15)

Orange Circle: AWARE OF GOD BUT INDIFFERENT TO HIM. God is not a priority compared to other preferred activities or goals. Feel they can make it on their own without a focus on God or a church community, may pray and go to church occasionally. Ecclesiastes 2:18-26) Mark 4: 25 Mathew 7: 7

Dark Blue Circle: ACCEPT GOD BUT ARE COMPLACENT. You believe in God. Attend church regularly, tithe, perform charitable works, are considered to be a good Christian people. Feel that following the rules leads to salvation. (Luke 15: 11-32) (2 Peter 1: 5-8) (Mathew 19: 16-28)

Light Blue Circle: DESIRE TO LEARN MORE ABOUT CHRIST. You take the initiative to grow in faith. You may participate in daily devotions, study the word of God, join small prayer groups or take part in religious church activities. (Luke 10: 38-42) (Proverbs 30: 5-6) (Mathew 18:19-20) (Isaiah 55: 6-11) (James 1:2-7) (Luke 6: 48-49) (Proverbs 2: 1-11) (Isaiah 41; 10)

Lavender Circle: DESIRE TO KNOW CHRIST IN A MORE PERSONAL WAY. You are taking dedicated time to focus on God and your relationship with Him. You have the desire to strengthen your faith and seek opportunities that will provide spiritual growth.(John 3:1-8) (Mathew 6: 25-28) (Isaiah 6: 8)

Gold Circle: DESIRE TO BE MORE LIKE CHRIST. You are exemplifying Christ's love for all through your life and the way you faithfully respond to His call. (James 1: 22-27) (Romans 10: 8-15) (Mathew 5: 13-16) (Mark 4: 26-32) (Mathew 13:1-9, 30-32) (1 Corinthians 3: 7-9) (1 Corinthians 13: 13)

Red Circle: EXUDE GOD'S LOVE. You are now embracing God as the center of your life. You are one with Christ. You act in Him, for Him and with Him in all that you do. (Isaiah 41: 10) (Luke 10:1-7) (Mathew 28:18-20) (Philippians 2: 12-18) (Colossians 3: 10-17)

Chapter III -- Outside of the Circles

UNAWARE OF OR REJECT GOD. This position is characterized by a disregard for God due to lack of knowledge, defiance or disinterest in Him. Total focus may be on money, fame, prestige, power, family, sports or recreation etc.

All of us are on our own personal journey including those on the outside of the circles.

All of us know family members, friends and others that are outside the circles. Perhaps we are there now or have been there in the past.

When many of us were growing up, we may have resented our father for disciplining us. We may not have realized that he was doing it out of love and concern for us. Now that we are fully grown adults, we may try to avoid God so that we can do as we please. To God the Father we are still His children. He loves us and is concerned about us and we need Him to guide us just as our earthly father guided us. The problem is: the Lord wants to help us and lead us more than we want to be helped or led. When we get rebuked for wrong doing instead of turning toward Him, we make excuses that lead us away from Him. If we look toward Him, we see our error in judgment and how to properly respond.

Hebrews 12:6-7

[6] because the Lord disciplines the one he loves, and he chastens everyone he accepts as his son.[7] Endure hardship as discipline; God is treating you as his children. For what children are not disciplined by their father?

Those who avoid God are not locked into this position. Until the very end there is hope that at some point we or they will realize something is missing and seek the Lord.

If we know God and want to help people along, we have things that we can do as the Lord implies in these gospels of Matthew and Mark.

Matthew 9: 1-7

[1] Getting into a boat, Jesus crossed over *the sea* and came to His own city.[2] and they brought to Him a paralytic lying on a bed. Seeing their faith, Jesus said to the paralytic, "Take courage, son; your sins are forgiven." [3] And some of the scribes said to themselves, "This *fellow* blasphemes." [4] And Jesus knowing their thoughts said, "Why are you thinking evil in your hearts? [5] Which is easier, to say, 'Your sins are forgiven,' or to say, 'Get up, and walk'? [6] But so that you may know that the Son of Man has

authority on earth to forgive sins"—then He *said to the paralytic, "Get up, pick up your bed and go home." ⁷ And he got up and went home.

Mark 2: 1-12

¹ When He had come back to Capernaum several days afterward, it was heard that He was at home. ² And many were gathered together, so that there was no longer room, not even near the door; and He was speaking the word to them. ³ And they came, bringing to Him a paralytic, carried by four men. ⁴ Being unable to get to Him because of the crowd, they removed the roof above Him; and when they had dug an opening, they let down the pallet on which the paralytic was lying. ⁵ And Jesus seeing their faith said to the paralytic, "Son, your sins are forgiven." ⁶ But some of the scribes were sitting there and reasoning in their hearts, ⁷ "Why does this man speak that way? He is blaspheming; who can forgive sins but God alone?" ⁸ Immediately Jesus, aware in His spirit that they were reasoning that way within themselves, said to them, "Why are you reasoning about these things in your hearts? ⁹ Which is easier, to say to the paralytic, 'Your sins are forgiven'; or to say, 'Get up, and pick up your pallet and walk'? ¹⁰ But so that you may know that the Son of Man has authority on earth to forgive sins"—He said to the paralytic, ¹¹ "I say to you, get up, pick up your pallet and go home." ¹² And he got up and immediately picked up the pallet and went out in the sight of everyone, so that they were all amazed and were glorifying God, saying, "We have never seen anything like this."

In both of these gospels Jesus cures paralytics, but first He forgives their sins and then he heals them. He does this to separate forgiveness of sins from healing.

Jesus attributes the healing and forgiveness to the faith of those who brought the paralytics to Him. What this implies is that our faith, prayers and actions can make a difference in the lives of others to the very end. Many people are not lost, they just have not been receptive to Christ as of yet. Prayers for the sick can be for both physical recovery and spiritual well being.

In addition to prayer, we can also plant seeds for the Lord. Planting seeds or evangelization is not that difficult if we think about sharing our faith with others. You can ask a friend to join you in a prayer group or ask them if they would like to go to Bible study with you. If there is someone with whom you would like to go on a retreat, ask them if they would like to join you. If you volunteer for service work, ask someone if they would like to go with you to help out.

It all starts with a question. Questions plant seeds. Remember, no matter what the response is from the person we asked, the seed has been planted, and the Lord will take it from there. I will give you examples as we get deeper into the book. Like the mustard seed, God can take the smallest of seeds and make them grow. If the seeds do not take hold and your prayers do not seem to work, it may not be God's time. Hope endures to the very end.

James 5: 13-16

¹³ Is anyone among you in trouble? Let them pray. Is anyone happy? Let them sing songs of praise. ¹⁴ Is anyone among you sick? Let them call the elders of the church to pray over them and anoint them with oil in the name of the Lord. ¹⁵ And the prayer offered in faith will make the sick person well; the Lord will raise them up. If they have sinned, they will be forgiven. ¹⁶ Therefore confess your sins to each other and pray for each other so that you may be healed. The prayer of a righteous person is powerful and effective.

Keep in mind that the people outside of the **orange** circle are not bad people. It is just that their main focus is on worldly things, maybe even very good things like devotion to family or a career, and they just don't even think about God. The focus of these people is elsewhere, and they do not have time or a desire to seek the Lord. Perhaps they were never really exposed to a Christian way of life.

If they are hostile, they may feel justified by unfortunate circumstances from the past, like bad personal experiences or even things that happened to friends, family or a group of people. Many things can drive them away from God. To guide them you must know where they are coming from and determine if they have any desire at all to seek the Lord. Whatever the situation, unless they have a desire, a significant emotional event or an awakening by the Spirit, they will be difficult to reach. I asked myself. "Is it possible for one to revive one's faith from outside the Circles?" I thought of the song *Amazing Grace* and it seemed unlikely without God's grace. Ponder the words from John Newton's song from Amazing Grace.

> Amazing grace! How sweet the sound that saved a wretch like me! I once was lost, but now am found; Was blind, but now I see.
>
> 'Twas grace that taught my heart to fear, And grace my fears relieved; How precious did that grace appear The hour I first believed.
>
> Through many dangers, toils and snares, I have already come; 'Tis grace hath brought me safe thus far, And grace will lead me home.
>
> The Lord has promised good to me, His Word my hope secures; He will my Shield and Portion be, As long as life endures.
>
> Yea, when this flesh and heart shall fail, And mortal life shall cease I shall possess, within the veil, a life of joy and peace.
>
> The earth shall soon dissolve like snow, The sun forbear to shine; But God, who called me here below, Will be forever mine.
>
> When we've been there ten thousand years, Bright shining as the sun, We've no less days to sing God's praise Than when we'd first begun.

Questions for self-reflection or group discussion:

How can anyone come to know the almighty God?
_____

_____

Do you believe that God made you to know, love and serve H?
_____

Do you believe there is life after death?
_____

What is the purpose of my life?
_____

_____

_____

Do you think you can influence people outside the circles?
_____

_____

What are your experiences and thoughts related to people outside of the circles?

Chapter IV -- Inside the Orange Circle

AWARE OF GOD BUT INDIFFERENT TO HIM. These people pray and go to church occasionally. God is not a priority compared to other preferred activities or goals. Their major focus may still be on money, fame, prestige, power, family, sports or recreation, etc.

This circle has many who call themselves Christians and have a life line to the church every Christmas or Easter. We may have been here after we left home, when we were young, before we started to seek the Lord or before we met our spouse. Their faith is weak at best, but they call on the Lord when they need a parachute in times of trouble. Over time they may find a need for Him or recognize that a void exists in their life which cannot be filled by career, family or other activities. They may be seeking God to help make things go their way. In the process the Lord starts to awaken them and if they respond, He will continue to draw them to Him.

It is interesting that we finally turn to God when times are especially difficult. That's often when we begin to pray. What we pray for is not necessarily what God knows is best for us. If it is not part of His plan, we may struggle until we are willing to relinquish control and turn it over completely to Him. God never gives up on us, and if we are open to seeking Him, we will eventually find Him. The key is to have the desire within to seek Him. To move from the **orange** circle we must have this desire.

My friend had the desire. Only he and the Lord knew why he was struggling. All I know is that the Spirit nurtured the seed that was planted during our discussion.

Ecclesiastes 2: 18-26

18 Thus I hated all the fruit of my labor for which I had labored under the sun, for I must leave it to the man who will come after me. 19 And who knows whether he will be a wise man or a fool? Yet he will have control over all the fruit of my labor for which I have labored by acting wisely under the sun. This too is vanity. 20 Therefore I completely despaired of all the fruit of my labor for which I had labored under the sun. 21 When there is a man who has labored with wisdom, knowledge and skill, then he gives his legacy to one who has not labored with them. This too is vanity and a great evil. 22 For what does a man get in all his labor and in his striving with which he labors under the sun? 23 Because all his days his task is painful and grievous; even at night his mind does not rest. This too is vanity.

[24] There is nothing better for a man *than* to eat and drink and tell himself that his labor is good. This also I have seen that it is from the hand of God. [25] For who can eat and who can have enjoyment without Him? [26] For to a person who is good in His sight He has given wisdom and knowledge and joy, while to the sinner He has given the task of gathering and collecting so that he may give to one who is good in God's sight. This too is vanity and striving after wind.

We often think of those inside the **orange** circle as un-churched because they spend so little time involved with their faith. In reality their focus is elsewhere, or they do not feel they get anything out of church. Church is something they feel slightly obligated to do. When we are not growing spiritually, our faith and belief in God diminishes until it becomes less and less important to us.

Perhaps this is a good time to ask ourselves. Why do we go to church? There may be a number of reasons. For Example:

- We want to put aside our daily tasks to take time for both immediate family and the family of God in our community.

- We know that if we are not part of a community of believers that our faith will die like a single dying ember. We cannot walk the path alone.

- We may go to be renewed by His presence in the Eucharist, the body and blood of Christ, so that we can be transformed.

- We may attend to listen to the gospel, to gain insight from the preaching and to hear God's small voice in meditation.
- We may want to praise God and worship with the community of like believers.
- We may go to pray in a Spiritual environment where we know He is present.

While people in the **orange** circle do not attend church very often, after meeting most of their goals, they may start to search for something more. They look at people around them who are at peace and wonder what they have to do to attain it.

Tim's story is one example of how the Lord calls someone far away to seek Him.

A number of years ago a friend of mine called and wanted to meet me for lunch. During lunch he said, "I want what you have before I have to have it." I said, "Tim what are you talking about?" He said,"I want to find God before I have to find Him." He said that he has seen a lot of people searching for God when they got cancer or something major had befallen them.

It was then that I told him about a three day program that I attended called Cum Christo, which is for both Catholics and Protestants. There is also a Cursillo weekend which is just for Catholics and an Emmaus weekend for Protestants. I told him I attended the weekend and found Christ there. In addition I discovered the depth of God's love for me. I then invited Tim to make a weekend. He accepted the invitation and three weeks later he made his Cum Christo weekend.

When I asked him how the weekend went, he said, "It was great, but I got into an argument with the people at my table." He said, "I told them my wife comes first and they said that God comes first." I said, "Tim they were right. God always wants what's best for you, and humans can't be depended upon like God can. If God comes first, everything else falls in place."

Less than 6 weeks later, Tim called me crying. He worked for a large retail supplier and, while visiting a client at the mall, saw his wife coming out of a Victoria's Secret store with another man. He approached them and an argument ensued. She then told him she wanted a divorce.

I believe God had sent Tim to me because He knew what was about to happen. Before he came to me at lunch that day, Tim and I had never talked about faith at all.

Tim met a pastor at Cum Christo and developed a relationship with other Christian men there. He started meeting with them and they helped him through this difficult period. Tim had his wife as his god. How devastating it can be when we have put all of our faith in something or someone, only to be let down.

Tim was in the **orange** circle, but came to know Christ. That was 20 years ago and he has had many more ups and downs, but he depends on God to help him through them and has continued to grow in his faith and trust in God. He still to this day meets with the small group he joined following his Cum Christo weekend, and they have helped him to progress on his walk.

Cum Christo is more than a retreat. It provides a method for a continuous and progressive conversion with a small group of friends.

What this story tells us is that when God intercedes, it does not take long for people to move out of the **orange** circle. It also tells us that just by living your faith, friends feel comfortable talking to you about faith matters, especially when prompted by the Spirit.

Someone will move from the **orange** circle to the **dark blue** only if they have an inner desire to do so. We may feel our children or friends are in the **orange** circle and nothing we do or say will encourage them to make the choices we feel would make a difference in their lives. All we can do is pray that they will accept the love of the Father and realize that it is up to them to seek what can only be found in Him.

Mark 4: 25

"For whoever has, to him more shall be given; and whoever does not have, even what he has shall be taken away from him."

Matthew 7:7

"Ask and it will be given to you; seek and you will find; knock and the door will be opened to you.

If you have family and friends outside or inside the **orange** circle, it helps to know why they are rejecting God. Knowing their position enables you to understand them and may provide a means to minister to them. Be a good listener. You are looking for understanding, not to convert or rebut their position.

Questions for self-reflection or group discussion:

Thinking about the orange circle, what can you do to encourage others you love to seek Christ?

_____

_____

_____

_____

Have you had any experiences where Christ used you to bring someone who was floundering into a closer relationship with Him?

_____

_____

_____

Have you had discussions related to faith with others inside or outside the **orange** circle? What was the response?

_____

_____

_____

What are your experiences and thoughts related to the orange circle?

Chapter V -- Inside the Dark Blue Circle

ACCEPT GOD BUT ARE COMPLACENT. These people feel that solely following the rules leads to salvation. They may go to church every Sunday, tithe, and perform charitable works. They are good people, but they do not make the extra effort to get to know Christ in a personal way.

The Prodigal son is a parable familiar to most of us.

Luke 15: 11-32

11 And He said, "A man had two sons. 12 The younger of them said to his father, "Father, give me the share of the estate that falls to me." So he divided his wealth between them. 13 And not many days later, the younger son gathered everything together and went on a journey into a distant country, and there he squandered his estate with loose living. 14 Now when he had spent everything, a severe famine occurred in that country and he began to be impoverished. 15 So he went and hired himself out to one of the citizens of that country, and he sent him into his fields to feed swine. 16 And he would have gladly filled his sTimach

with the pods that the swine were eating, and no one was giving *anything* to him. [17] But when he came to his senses, he said, 'How many of my father's hired men have more than enough bread, but I am dying here with hunger! [18] I will get up and go to my father, and will say to him, "Father, I have sinned against heaven, and in your sight; [19]I am no longer worthy to be called your son; make me as one of your hired men."' [20] So he got up and came to his father. But while he was still a long way off, his father saw him and felt compassion *for him*, and ran and embraced him and kissed him. [21] And the son said to him, "Father, I have sinned against heaven and in your sight; I am no longer worthy to be called your son." [22] But the father said to his slaves, "Quickly bring out the best robe and put it on him, and put a ring on his hand and sandals on his feet; [23] and bring the fattened calf, kill it, and let us eat and celebrate; [24] for this son of mine was dead and has come to life again; he was lost and has been found." And they began to celebrate.[25] "Now his older son was in the field, and when he came and approached the house, he heard music and dancing. [26] And he summoned one of the servants and *began* inquiring what these things could be. [27] And he said to him, "Your brother has come, and your father has killed the fattened calf because he has received him back safe and sound." [28] But he became angry and was not willing to go in; and his father came out and *began* pleading with him. [29] But he answered and said to his father, "Look! For so many years I have been serving you and I have never neglected a command of yours; and *yet* you have never given me a young goat, so that I might celebrate with my friends; [30] but when this son of yours came, who has devoured your wealth with prostitutes, you killed the fattened calf for him." [31] And he said to him, "Son, you have always been with me, and all that is mine is yours. [32] But we had to celebrate and rejoice, for this brother of yours was dead and *has begun* to live, and *was* lost and has been found."

Both sons are lost but only one knows it. The younger son was in the **orange** circle but returns with a desire to be with the Father. He is moving into the **dark blue circle**.

The interesting thing about this story is that the older son was in the **dark blue** circle. He has always been with the father. He is like someone going to church every Sunday as a sense of duty. The elder son feels that through his loyalty, he is entitled to everything the father has. But he has not moved to a close relationship with his father. He has not shared the father's love. He has not yet started to move toward being one with the Father. He is stuck in the **dark blue** circle. He has not embraced going beyond self to know his father's will or his father's love for him.

The hardest circle to break through is the **dark blue**. Many of us were brought up to believe that if we went to church each Sunday, obeyed the commandments, and did good works, we would be in heaven. As we review the circles and scripture, we may see that more is required than what we originally thought to earn a place in heaven.

Many of us have been or are in the **dark blue** circle. As I said before, I was in it for 26 years and would probably still be, if someone hadn't asked me to make a Cursillo weekend. Cursillo was the start of my journey to a closer relationship with God. It was a gift from God, and like any gift, we can only discover its value once we open it. I opened the gift, but not all accept the invitation. It could be due to fear of change, complacency, self righteousness or maybe they are just not yet ready to commit. There are of course other ways to discover Christ's love for us, but this was the door I opened.

I encourage you to accept the Lord's invitation to grow in your faith and spirituality in any form that is offered. It may be Bible study, a Cursillo weekend, retreats or mission work, etc. Do not be afraid to open the gifts the Lord presents through others.

When you say "yes" to the Lord, you will be given spiritual gifts. Paul notes what some of these spiritual gifts are in his letter to the Corinthians.

1 Corinthians 12: 4-11

[4] There are different kinds of gifts, but the same Spirit distributes them. [5] There are different kinds of service, but the same Lord. [6] There are different kinds of working, but in all of them and in everyone it is the same God at work. [7] Now to each one the manifestation of the Spirit is given for the common good. [8] To one there is given through the Spirit a message of wisdom, to another a message of knowledge by means of the same Spirit, [9] to another faith by the same Spirit, to another gifts of healing by that one Spirit, [10] to another miraculous powers, to another prophecy, to another distinguishing between spirits, to another speaking in different kinds of tongues, and to still another the interpretation of tongues. [11] All these are the work of one and the same

Spirit, and he distributes them to each one, just as he determines.

Beyond spiritual gifts we have personal gifts. Some are noted in:

2 Peter 1: 5-8

[5] For this very reason, make every effort to add to your faith goodness; and to goodness, knowledge; [6] and to knowledge, self-control; and to self-control, perseverance; and to perseverance, godliness; [7] and to godliness, mutual affection; and to mutual affection, love. [8] For if you possess these qualities in increasing measure, they will keep you from being ineffective and unproductive in your knowledge of our Lord Jesus Christ.

There are a multitude of other gifts, which we call virtues. I suggest you Google virtues and list those with which you have been blessed. God will bestow many more of these virtues or gifts upon those who ask for them to enable them to serve Him. Take time to identify those he has already given you and those you would like to receive. You will be amazed at how uplifting this can be. You will see how good God is. Then ask yourself. "Am I using my personal gifts for God's purposes?"

James 1: 19-26

[19] My dear brothers and sisters, take note of this: Everyone should be quick to listen, slow to speak and slow to become angry, [20] because human anger does not produce the righteousness that God desires. [21] Therefore, get rid of all moral filth and the evil that is

so prevalent and humbly accept the word planted in you, which can save you.

[22] Do not merely listen to the word, and so deceive yourselves. Do what it says. [23] Anyone who listens to the word but does not do what it says is like someone who looks at his face in a mirror [24] and, after looking at himself, goes away and immediately forgets what he looks like. [25] But whoever looks intently into the perfect law that gives freedom, and continues in it—not forgetting what they have heard, but doing it—they will be blessed in what they do.

[26] Those who consider themselves religious and yet do not keep a tight rein on their tongues deceive themselves, and their religion is worthless. [27] Religion that God our Father accepts as pure and faultless is this: to look after orphans and widows in their distress and to keep oneself from being polluted by the world.

Hebrews 3: 12-15

[12] See to it, brothers and sisters, that none of you has a sinful, unbelieving heart that turns away from the living God. [13] But encourage one another daily, as long as it is called "Today," so that none of you may be hardened by sin & deceitfulness. [14] We have come to share in Christ, if indeed we hold our original conviction firmly to the very end. [15] As has just been said: "Today, if you hear his voice, do not harden your hearts as you did in the rebellion."

God has something for each of us to do. What is more, you already know what it is. As the Nike commercial says, "Just do it." Today is the day. Today comes every day, but happiness today comes from doing God's will.

Questions for self-reflection or group discussion:

Have you been or are you in the blue circle?

_____

How deep is your relationship with Christ at this time?

_____

There are many gifts. What gifts do you feel you have?

_____

_____

In our care for others or the church, do we use our gifts from God out of love of Him or for our own self satisfaction?

_____

One question we all must try to answer is: Where does God want me to be at this time? The answer is seldom where we are currently at.

One small step in our faith walk could turn into a giant leap. What do you think the next step on your journey ought to be?

_____

What are your experiences and thoughts for your story?

Chapter VI -- Inside the Light Blue Circle

DESIRE TO LEARN MORE ABOUT CHRIST. In this circle the person takes the initiative to grow in his or her faith by daily devotion, being active in studying the word of God, joining small prayer groups, doing Bible study or attending religious church activities.

Many vacillate between the **dark blue** and the **light blue** circles. However, those in the **light blue** are being drawn into a closer relationship with Christ. They have a thirst for knowledge and understanding. The Spirit uses God's word, study, books, and other people to quench this thirst. When we join with others and share our thoughts, we all get different perspectives to enlighten us. In this circle we will focus on scripture to get to know about Christ.

The familiar story about Martha and Mary is revealing.

Luke 10: 38-42

³⁸ As Jesus and his disciples were on their way, he came to a village where a woman named Martha opened her home to him. ³⁹ She had a sister called Mary, who sat at the Lord's feet listening to what he said. ⁴⁰ But Martha was distracted by all the preparations that had to be made. She came to him and asked, "Lord, don't you care that my sister has left me to do the work by myself? Tell her to help me!"

⁴¹ "Martha, Martha," the Lord answered, "you are worried and upset about many things, ⁴² but only one thing is needed. Mary has chosen what is better, and it will not be taken away from her."

One of the things Christ is saying here is that what Martha is doing is expected and admired by people of the day and even today. Martha is in the **dark blue** circle. She is doing what is expected and doing good and necessary things with her time, but she is too busy to spend time to listen to Christ. She does not take advantage of this opportunity God has given her to grow spiritually. She is missing out on His teaching and His very presence. She may never have another opportunity like this to get to know Him. When she asks Jesus for help, He says, "Martha, Martha you are concerned about many things, but Mary has chosen a better thing and it will not be taken from her."

We are often like Martha in that we have a lot of opportunities to hear the word of God beyond Sunday, like an occasional day long or evening program. Take advantage of them to grow in knowledge, understanding and spirituality.

Anyone who has taken a Bible study course knows that the message could have several meanings. Through Bible study you are exposed to Bible scholars or others to whom the Spirit has provided additional insight. The Spirit does reveal what He wants you to learn based upon where you are in your walk, but He often reveals it through others in a group such as Bible study or a small prayer group. With different insights we look deeper. Belonging to a small study group can provide insight as well as the self-discipline we all need to continue to grow in our faith and a closer relationship with the Lord.

As I gained more insight from Bible study, I found the prayer of St. Ephraim thoughtful and inspirational.

Prayer of St. Ephraim

>Lord, who can grasp all the wealth of just one of your words? What we understand is much less than we leave behind, like thirsty people who drink from a fountain. For your word, Lord, has many shades of meaning just as those who study it have many different points of view. The Lord has colored his word with many hues so that each person who studies it can see in it what he loves. He has hidden many treasures in his word so that each of us is enriched as we meditate on it.

>The word of God is a tree of life that from all its parts offers you fruit that is blessed. It is like that rock opened in the desert that from all its parts gave forth a spiritual drink. He who comes into contact with some share of its treasure should not think that the only thing contained in the word is what he

himself has found. He should realize that he has only been able to find that one thing from among many others. Nor, because only that one part has become his, should he say that the word is void and empty and look down on it. But because he could not exhaust it, he should give thanks for its riches. Be glad that you are overcome and do not be sad that it overcame you. The thirsty man rejoices when he drinks and he is not downcast because he cannot empty the fountain. Rather let the fountain quench your thirst than have your thirst quench the fountain. Because if your thirst is quenched and the fountain is not exhausted, you can drink from it again whenever you are thirsty. But if when your thirst is quenched and the fountain is also dried up, your victory will bode evil for you.

So be grateful for what you have received and don't grumble about the abundance left behind. What you have received and what you have reached is your share. What remains is your heritage. What at one time you were unable to receive because of your weakness, you will be able to receive at other times if you persevere. Do not have the presumption to try to take in one draft what cannot be taken in one draft and do not abandon out of laziness what can only be taken little by little.

The word of the Lord does not change, but our understanding and insight do as we grow spiritually.

Proverbs 30: 5

⁵"Every word of God is flawless; he is a shield to those who take refuge in him."

Matthew 18: 19-20

¹⁹"Again, truly I tell you that if two of you on earth agree about anything they ask for, it will be done for them by my Father in heaven. ²⁰ For where two or three gather in my name, there am I with them."

The Bible tells us that coming to a close relationship with the Lord is a process and a journey with many difficult obstacles that we must overcome. These obstacles are primarily self-imposed, such as complacency, busyness, false ideals of happiness and self-righteousness.

Isaiah 41:10.

So do not fear, for I am with you; do not be dismayed, for I am your God. I will strengthen you and help you; I will uphold you with my righteous right hand.

Isaiah 55: 1-11

¹ "Come, all you who are thirsty, come to the waters; and you who have no money, come, buy and eat! Come; buy wine and milk without money and without cost. ² Why spend money on what is not bread, and your labor on what does not satisfy?

Listen, listen to me, and eat what is good and you will delight in the richest of fare. Give ear and come to me; listen, that you may live. I will make an everlasting covenant with you, my faithful love promised to David. ⁴ See, I have made him a witness to the peoples, a ruler and commander of the peoples. ⁵

Surely you will summon nations you know not, and nations you do not know will come running to you, because of the Lord your God, the Holy One of Israel, for he has endowed you with splendor." 6 Seek the Lord while he may be found; call on him while he is near. 7 Let the wicked forsake their ways and the unrighteous their thoughts. Let them turn to the Lord, and he will have mercy on them, and to our God, for he will freely pardon. 8 "For my thoughts are not your thoughts, neither are your ways my ways," declares the Lord. 9"As the heavens are higher than the earth, so are my ways higher than your ways and my thoughts than your thoughts. 10As the rain and the snow come down from heaven, and do not return to it without watering the earth and making it bud and flourish, so that it yields seed for the sower and bread for the eater, 11so is my word that goes out from my mouth: It will not return to me empty, but will accomplish what I desire and achieve the purpose for which I sent it.

In the process of getting to know Christ, we come to a deeper faith and a desire for a closer relationship with Him. We need perseverance to overcome obstacles which resurface when we start to drift away.

James (1: 2-7)

2 Consider it pure joy, my brothers and sisters, whenever you face trials of many kinds, 3 because you know that the testing of your faith produces perseverance. 4 Let perseverance finish its work so that you may be mature and complete, not lacking anything. 5 if any of you lacks wisdom, you should ask God, who gives generously to all without finding fault, and it will be given to you. 6 But when you ask, you

must believe and not doubt, because the one who doubts is like a wave of the sea, blown and tossed by the wind. ⁷ That person should not expect to receive anything from the Lord. Such a person is double-minded and unstable in all they do.

Faith and trust in God are requirements when seeking God's help. In my friend's story which prompted the concept of the circles, it appears that his desires may not have been what God wanted. Before God can provide anything, we must first submit freely to His will. Then God can provide what we need, which is not necessarily what we think is best. In almost any stage of our spiritual growth. God's will is seldom clear, but in Proverbs we get guidance.

Proverbs 2: 1-11

¹My son, if you accept my words and store up my commands within you, ² turning your ear to wisdom and applying your heart to understanding— ³ indeed, if you call out for insight and cry aloud for understanding,⁴ and if you look for it as for silver and search for it as for hidden treasure ⁵ then you will understand the fear of the LORD and find the knowledge of God. ⁶ For the LORD gives wisdom; from his mouth come knowledge and understanding. ⁷ He holds success in store for the upright he is a shield to those whose walk is blameless, ⁸ for he guards the course of the just and protects the way of his faithful ones.⁹ Then you will understand what is right and just and fair—every good path. ¹⁰ For wisdom will enter your heart, and knowledge will be pleasant to your soul. ¹¹ Discretion will protect you, and understanding will guard you.

Questions for self-reflection or group discussion:

What programs are offered at your church, for education or spiritual growth?

_____

Most churches have small study groups that we are not aware of. Ask people at church or your religious education director if they know how you might join one.

What programs do other churches in the area provide?

_____

_____

Does your church provide spiritual renewal programs such as New Life, CHIRP or Cursillo?

_____

Does your church have organizations which would interest you, like Stephen Ministry, social justice, a mom's group or men's group?

_____

How much time do you spend trying to determine God's will, in meditation, prayer and study?

What are your experiences and thoughts for your story?

Chapter VII -- Inside the Lavender Circle

DESIRE TO KNOW CHRIST IN A MORE PERSONAL WAY. These people set aside dedicated time to focus on God and have a relationship with Him. Examples would be adoration, pilgrimages or taking advantage of other spiritual environments. The most impactful are often three day retreats such as, Cursillo, Emmaus, etc., which provide a process for any Christian to stay on track in their walk and accountability.

Once you know about Christ, it is easier to move into a deeper relationship with Him. As you spend more time with Him, you become more open to the Spirit's prompting. Many of you are reading this because you have a desire to know Jesus in a personal way or you already know Him in a personal way and want to continue to grow in your faith. Christ's grace is prompting you to come closer to Him. Many of you have gone on retreats which provide an atmosphere in which to pray and listen to the word of the Lord, and then reflect upon it. There is great value in this. Some of you may not yet have a close relationship with Christ but are seeking to get to know Him. It is when you spend dedicated time to grow spiritually closer to Him that you do indeed come to know him in a new way.

Knowing about Christ is not the same as knowing Him.

Pope Benedict said in his year of faith address, "Dear brothers and sisters, this is true for every Christian. Faith is first and foremost a personal intimate encounter with Jesus. It is having an experience of His closeness, His friendship and His love. It is in this way that we learn to know Him even better, to love Him and to follow Him more and more. May this happen to each one of us."[2]

This closeness Pope Benedict is talking about starts with the Holy Spirit creating a desire within each of us to seek a more personal relationship with Christ.

Retreat centers for spiritual renewal are available throughout the United States. Dedicated time spent with Christ in solitude is always grace filled, allowing the Lord to speak to us directly. On a larger scale there are trips to the Holy Land or pilgrimages. One of the most impactful pilgrimages is to the Holy Land

---

2. Excerpts from Cardinal Ratzinger's year of faith address "The Easter Miracle" Pentecost 1998.

under the direction of a biblical scholar. Regionally, monasteries and retreat centers also offer day, weekend and longer programs for education and renewal.

Someone asked what was so impactful for me on my Cursillo. It is difficult to explain, but the next couple of pages attempt to explain it.

Cursillo is a three-day weekend, started in Spain in the 1940's by lay people to revitalize a dying church. The Cursillo through a series of 15 talks, each building upon another, provides a foundation for a progressive and continuous conversion. As the weekend unfolds those attending come to a deeper realization of how much God loves them.

The value of making a three-day weekend like Cursillo, Emmaus, Tres Dias or Cum Christo, is that while they can be a mountain top experience in your life, they usually are the beginning of a new life of faith. The Cursillo method provides spiritual growth through small friendship groups who share their journey together.

Think of your faith as being an ember in the fireplace. When the fire is hot, you glow along with all the other embers. Then as the fire dies down your ember loses some of the glow. As long as there are other embers next to you, you all manage to keep the fire burning. But, if you get separated from the other embers, your glow starts to dim and eventually dies. Now if a couple of embers come next to you again, your glow comes alive. The fire rekindles and begins to burn again. This is what happens with our faith life. If we share it with a small group of friends, it continues to grow and glow, if not, it dies. We cannot keep our faith alive unless we meet with like minded friends. On the three-day weekend you are encouraged to keep your ember or faith alive by meeting with Spirit filled friends on the same journey to salvation.

A testimony for Cursillo was written in the January 2015 issue of the *Catholic Telegraph.* Auxiliary Bishop Joseph Binzer of the Cincinnati Diocese was quoted in an article written by John Stegeman, called "My Journey." In the article Bishop Binzer noted how crucial Cursillo was to his faith development as a young man.

He said, "Cursillo is a 72-hour retreat of sorts with prayer, speakers, and sacraments, as well as follow up events." Bishop Binzer credits his Cursillo for helping him to recognize God's love.

"I would call it a moment, and I've had many moments like these, when God enlightened me about how much God loved me." Bishop Binzer said, "That came through the men who were on the weekend, team members and other people making their Cursillo."

Prior to his Cursillo, Bishop Binzer prayed daily and attended Mass on weekends. Afterwards, his faith life began to take on more focus. "There was more of an understanding of what the purpose of my life should be," he said.

According to the article, Bishop Binzer, who describes himself as one not prone to taking risks, talked his brother into attending Cursillo with him. He now encourages Catholics seeking to grow in their faith to try something outside their own comfort zones.

"I think the thing to do would be to try something you haven't tried before and to listen to what God might be calling you to, and to accept an invitation to do something spiritually in the Catholic Church you haven't done before," referencing opportunities such as Cursillo, Bible studies, parish education events and more.

Most people at one time or another ask themselves this question. Isn't there more of a purpose for my life on this earth? Some seek to discover the answer.

Many people struggle with their belief in God. If you have a desire to discover if God exists and search for the truth you will find Him.

The following story is an example of someone trying to find if God exists, and she is responding to His call.

A woman, an agnostic (a person who does not have a definite belief in God), went to stay at the Abbey of Gethsemane in KY to see if indeed it provided anything at all. While there, she joined a number of men walking through the gardens and started asking them about why they came, what they hoped to gain by being there and what they had discovered so far. She came to the Abbey because she thought it might provide what she was looking for. What she discovered was a sense of peace and a greater desire than ever to discover the source of that peace. The men she joined were part of a Cursillo community seeking a time for personal solitude with Christ. Later she would tell them she did find peace being at the abbey.

A retreat is not the only place we can encounter Christ in a personal way. We can discover Him right in our parishes through evangelization. Evangelization is a scary word. The *Diocese of Camden.* clearly states what we need to do to bring our friends to Christ and how we might be evangelized by friends to bring us to Christ. If we have the desire to respond to what God asks of us, He will provide the strength and means to accomplish it.

Diocese of Camden NJ. Evangelization Definition

"Evangelization is not a program. It is to bring people into a relationship with Jesus" (Lifelong Faith Formation Director's Meeting – September 17, 2009).

We see evangelization as a continuous three-step process. We are invited to live this process and incorporate new parish members into this experience:

1. Discovering Jesus through a personal encounter with him.
2. Following Jesus, becoming his disciple.
3. Proclaiming the Good News is to be a witness of Jesus.

Many churches are living that definition, They are being revitalized through CHIRP (Christ Renews His Parish) and other Christ centered programs. For the youth there is the Net Ministries program where college students help parishes introduce youth to the living presence of Christ in a fun and exciting way. Most of our churches provide confirmation retreats. All of these programs are inspired by the Holy Spirit to help discover Christ in a new way. Below is an example.

In a November 18, 2012, church bulletin it was noted that an 8th grade class from Dayton, OH, while preparing for Confirmation, spent two full Sundays at the Bergamo Retreat Center. After the retreat they were asked to write a letter to God. The letters represented their struggles as young teenagers and the influence of their parents and peer groups. One letter had a message for all of us.

> Dear God:
>
> I can say that I have not taken my faith as seriously as I should have. I feel as if I've viewed my faith as just another thing to do. I viewed it as just another guideline or rulebook that I have to follow. Though today I have come to the realization that I shouldn't view my faith as something I have to do but instead something I get to do. I have realized that it is a blessing that I get to serve Jesus. It is a blessing to be able to have the opportunity to help and serve the less fortunate. In my opinion

faith isn't a guideline or a rulebook but instead it is a gift that God has given to us. We should cherish the opportunity that we have each day. We all have the same opportunity to change someone or something in a positive way. Through Confirmation we can only strengthen our faith, we can only build the desire to do good and to show love to everyone that we can.

Max [3]

Maybe we should take a look at ourselves and our faith. Do we look at it as a gift? Is it a privilege to serve the Lord? Do you know the Savior who died to redeem us and who has set aside a place for us with Him in Heaven?

When we read this we think, Wow!!, this is great for our youth. They really need this. But what about us? Are we too old and established for a retreat? I do not think we can be too old or too young to spend time with Christ. All we need is the desire to spend quality time with Him and respond to the opportunities God provides.

Whenever we make an effort to spend one on one time with God, we are given the gift of grace because He wants us to have a personal relationship with Him. Everyone who answers the call to discover Christ takes a big step forward on their journey

---

[3] Church of the Incarnation bulletin November 18, 2012

because God's will and their will come together for that period of time.

Do you remember the story of Nicodemus in the Bible? He was a scholar of the Old Testament. He was familiar with God's teaching and would probably be considered close to God due to his knowledge. He knew about God, but the Holy Spirit was creating a desire within him to get to know Christ in a personal way.

John 3: 1-8

¹Now there was a Pharisee, a man named Nicodemus who was a member of the Jewish ruling council. 2 He came to Jesus at night and said, "Rabbi, we know that you are a teacher who has come from God. For no one could perform the signs you are doing if God were not with him." 3 Jesus replied, "Very truly I tell you, no one can see the kingdom of God unless they are born again." 4 "How can someone be born when they are old?" Nicodemus asked. "Surely they cannot enter a second time into their mother's womb to be born!" 5 Jesus answered, "Very truly I tell you, no one can enter the kingdom of God unless they are born of water and the Spirit. 6 Flesh gives birth to flesh, but the Spirit gives birth to spirit. 7 You should not be surprised at my saying, 'You must be born again.' 8 The wind blows wherever it pleases. You hear its sound, but you cannot tell where it comes from or where it is going. So it is with everyone born of the Spirit."

Today many learned people know about God and His teaching and yet they do not know Christ in a personal way.

Anything that gets in the way of a closer relationship with Christ is an obstacle that needs to be overcome. What obstacles may be in your life? Jesus tells us.

Matthew 6: 25-33

25 "Therefore I tell you, do not worry about your life, what you will eat or drink; or about your body, what you will wear. Is not life more than food, and the body more than clothes? 26 Look at the birds of the air; they do not sow or reap or store away in barns, and yet your heavenly Father feeds them. Are you not much more valuable than they? 27 Can any one of you by worrying add a single hour to your life[?

28 "And why do you worry about clothes? See how the flowers of the field grow. They do not labor or spin. 29 Yet I tell you that not even Solomon in all his splendor was dressed like one of these. 30 If that is how God clothes the grass of the field, which is here today and Timorrow is thrown into the fire, will he not much more clothe you—you of little faith? 31 So do not worry, saying, 'What shall we eat?' or 'What shall we drink?' or 'What shall we wear?' 32 For the pagans run after all these things, and your heavenly Father knows that you need them. 33 But seek first his kingdom and his righteousness, and all these things will be given to you as well. 34 Therefore do not worry about Timorrow, for Timorrow will worry about itself. Each day has enough trouble of its own".

In addition to removing any obstacles, we also need to take the initiative to seek God.

St. Ignatius tells us that if we do not venture forth in seeking God, we become complacent and lose our desire to put God first and lead others to Christ. The goal is to allow God to live in us so that through us He can save, console, heal and bring others to Him.

Isaiah 6: 8

Then I heard the voice of the Lord saying, "Whom shall I send? And who will go for us?"

And I said, "Here am I. Send me!"

To be sent we need to have a desire to be like Him. The goal of a virtuous life is to become like Christ.

We can acquire a multitude of virtues. A virtue is a habitual and firm disposition to do good. It allows the person not only to perform good acts, but to give the best of himself. The virtuous person tends toward the good with all his sensory and spiritual powers; he pursues the good and chooses it in concrete actions.

Philippians 4: 8

Finally, brothers and sisters, whatever is true, whatever is noble, whatever is right, whatever is pure, whatever is lovely, whatever is admirable—if anything is excellent or praiseworthy—think about such things.

Questions for self-reflection or group discussion:

How could the laity in your church accomplish bringing the good news and being the good news within the parish?

_____

What do you think of Bishop Binzer's idea of trying something you haven't tried before and listening to what God might be calling you to? Think about accepting an invitation to do something spiritually in your church which perhaps you have thought of doing but have not yet taken the initiative.

_____

_____

What deters Christians from seeking a closer relationship with Christ?

_____

_____

_____

_____

Do you feel you know Christ in a personal way?

_____

_____

If you already know Christ, do you think attending a weekend like Cursillo, Tres Dais Emmaus or Cum Christo would enhance your relationship with Him?

_____

Do you go beyond attending regular Sunday service to honor God or to increase your knowledge of Him?

_____

_____

_____

Love is expressed through the virtues we have. Think about that in depth; what virtues do you think you possess?

_____

_____

_____

Which virtues do you think you can more fully develop to bring Christ's love to others?

_____

_____

What are your experiences and thoughts for your story?

Chapter VIII -- Inside the Gold Circle

DESIRE TO BE MORE LIKE CHRIST. These people exemplify Christ's love for all in their thoughts, words and actions. They are faithful in responding to His call and going where He leads. They beg the Lord for grace to know Him more intimately, love Him more deeply and desire Him more closely.

Once you have gotten to know Christ in a personal way, you need to share the gifts you have received. If you do not share the gifts given to you, they will begin to diminish. To sustain the gifts, we need to spend time with the Lord. More importantly, we must share our gifts, realizing that what we do, we do for the Lord. We grow closer to Christ as we bring others to Him because he gives us grace, As we do his will, we become disciples in our circle of influence. Some, like the Diocese of Camden, call it evangelization.

Sometimes we evangelize without knowing it. This happens when by being Christians, others become aware of the presence of Christ in our lives and they are drawn to Him.

At other times we intentionally evangelize when we wish to have someone join us on our journey. We ask them to join us at Bible study, or to perhaps attend a function, or activity that would give them the opportunity to be exposed to the love of God.

Romans 10: 8-15

8 But what does it say? The word is near you; it is in your mouth and in your heart, that is, the message concerning faith that we proclaim: 9 If you declare with your mouth, "Jesus is Lord," and believe in your heart that God raised him from the dead, you will be saved. 10 For it is with your heart that you believe and are justified, and it is with your mouth that you profess your faith and are saved. 11 As Scripture says, "Anyone who believes in him will never be put to shame." 12 For there is no difference between Jew and Gentile—the same Lord is Lord of all and richly blesses all who call on him, 13 for, "Everyone who calls on the name of the Lord will be saved." 14 How, then, can they call on the one they have not believed in? And how can they believe in the one of whom they have not heard? And how can they hear without someone preaching to them? 15 And how can anyone preach unless they are sent? As it is written: "How beautiful are the feet of those who bring good news!"

Matthew 5: 13-16

¹³ "You are the salt of the earth; but if the salt has become tasteless, how can it be made salty *again*? It is no longer good for anything, except to be thrown out and trampled under-foot by men."

¹⁴ "You are the light of the world, a city set on a hill cannot be hidden; ¹⁵ nor does *anyone* light a lamp and put it under a basket, but on the lampstand, and it gives light to all who are in the house. ¹⁶ Let your light shine before men in such a way that they may see your good works, and glorify your Father who is in heaven."

Matthew 13: 1-9

¹That same day Jesus went out of the house and sat by the lake. ² Such large crowds gathered around him that he got into a boat and sat in it, while all the people stood on the shore. ³ Then he told them many things in parables, saying: "A farmer went out to sow his seed. ⁴ As he was scattering the seed, some fell along the path, and the birds came and ate it up. ⁵ Some fell on rocky places, where it did not have much soil. It sprang up quickly, because the soil was shallow. ⁶ But when the sun came up, the plants were scorched, and they withered because they had no root. ⁷ Other seed fell among thorns, which grew up and choked the plants. ⁸ Still other seed fell on good soil, where it produced a crop—a hundred, sixty or thirty times what was sown. ⁹ Whoever has ears, let them hear."

You bear fruit when you bring others to a realization that God is always with us. You do it through your words, actions and especially by having the courage to reach out in true friendship and ask someone to join you in your walk.

We are asked to sow seeds. This scares people, but all that is required is that you ask people close to you and around you to join you when the opportunity arises. Invite them to Bible study, or at a holy hour, invite them to go to church with you or on a retreat or to an educational program that is offered. How do you do it? Ask a simple question. Would you like to go with me?

If you use statements, the listeners can tune you out, but if you ask a question, they must take it into their mind to form a response. If they go with you, wonderful, if they say "no", the seed remains and with the Lord's help may germinate at a later date. No matter what circle you are in, you can make a difference.

Let me give you an example of how a simple question gave God the opportunity to change people's lives,

Mark's story

I was a sales manager at a company in Dayton. Mark came up from Atlanta for a quarterly review. He had expected us to go out to dinner that evening, but I had Bible study. So it came to me to ask him if he would like to join me. His first response was that he had an early morning meeting, to which I responded that I would be in that same meeting. He then said, "I don't have a Bible." I said. "Look in the drawer in your hotel room." He laughed and said, "I still do not want to go." That was that. For the next quarterly review, I traveled to Atlanta and he invited me to dinner at his home. After they put the children to bed, we took time to relax. Mark brought up the Bible study incident. I do not remember what was said, but we discussed Christ for over an hour. I left the next day.

Although we spoke about business almost every day, it was about two years later that he told me over the phone that I saved their marriage. I said, "Saved your marriage? I didn't even know you were having trouble." He then told me that when I visited them they had been in marriage counseling and that it wasn't working. After our talk they went to their priest and he suggested Retrouvaille. They went through it and were now teaching it. I had no idea what Retrouvaille was. He then explained that it was a program conducted by a spiritual director and lay people. The program is aimed at reconciling broken marriages by opening communications and putting Christ at the core in the marriage. Although a Catholic program, it is open to all denominations and they were now on a team to teach it.

Mark and I did not discuss our faith after that until 13 years later. After I left the company, I received a Christmas card from him. His closing on the card said, "Thank you for introducing me to Jesus. Give me a call." I called him a few days later and found he had come a long way in both his career and his faith.

Mark and his wife Linda were now attending Bible study and church regularly. He surprised me when he stated that he would like to get closer to Christ. I said, "You are in Bible study, you've conducted Retrouvaille where Christ is present and you attend church regularly." Then I realized that Christ had sent Mark to me to search out a way to develop a closer spiritual relationship. We discussed three day walks like Cursillo and Emmaus. Two months later I was his sponsor for an Emmaus weekend.

After the weekend, I picked him up and we went to his home where I was to spend the night. That evening when Mark got up to get some drinks, Linda asked Mark, "What was the walk like?" Mark said, "It was like Retrouvaille on steroids." Linda turned to me and said, "How can that be? How can that be? Retrouvaille saved our marriage. "I said, "With Retrouvaille there was you and there was Mark with Christ in the center. On his walk this last weekend, there was only Mark and Christ, so it was a much more personal encounter."

Linda had told me at lunch at the airport before Mark arrived that she thought the weekend would be good for him but she wasn't sure she wanted to go on one. (Many people feel that a spiritual weekend would be good for their spouse but that they aren't sure about themselves.), In the end Linda decided to go to the next weekend and had a marvelous and uplifting experience as well.

The following week I received an e-mail from Linda. It read, "I discovered how much God loves me and how much I love Him. Thanks for being persistent with me to follow Mark. You are an angel." After reading this to my wife and friends on vacation with us at the time, we all laughed because they knew me. But even here the Lord was working. Our friends, who were with us, asked about Cursillo and we sponsored them the following year.

We brushed off the angel comment in Linda's e-mail at the time. But recently the comment came back to mind when the celebrant at early morning Mass, discussed in his homily the hierarchy of angels. He made reference to the teaching of Pope Saint Gregory the Great (Second Reading of the Office of Reading on September 29th: Feast of the Archangels) that "the word 'angel' is the name of an office not of a nature." He said that angel means messenger.

He stated that humans can be angels when they are delivering a message to someone for God. We are all angels when we receive God's call and deliver His message. This is not hard to believe when we think about how often someone has made a comment like he or she was a God sent *angel*. Maybe the messenger showed up at just the right moment to help someone in a difficult situation, or maybe the messenger gave peaceful compassion when it was needed. Angels in this sense are carrying a God given message and the person receiving the message should have their spiritual life enhanced because of it. The love, peace, kindness or comfort should be attributed to God, not to the messenger. God is sending the message and showing His love and personal involvement in our and their daily lives.

God empowers His angels. He gives them the opportunity, the courage and the means to deliver the message. I learned through this homily that we never know when the Spirit is working through us or using us. As in Mark's case it all started with that simple question. "Would you like to go to Bible study with me?"

What if I hadn't responded to the Spirit's prompting? I could have reasoned, I don't even know what religion he is, he might feel uncomfortable, or he will probably say no. When I look back, I realize that if I had taken time to think about it, I probably would not have invited him. When the spirit encourages us to invite someone, we need to respond. We are called to plant the little seeds, the rest is up to God.

1 Corinthians 3: 7-9

7 So neither the one who plants nor the one who waters is anything, but only God, who makes things grow. 8 The one who plants and the one who waters have one purpose, and they will each be rewarded according to their own labor. 9 For we are co-workers in God's service; you are God's field, God's building.

If I hadn't invited Mark to Bible study, the discussion on Christ would not have come up to initiate saving the marriage. When I talked about the thank you e-mail from Linda with our friends, it led to discussing

Cursillo and eventually they made a Cursillo weekend.

Perhaps the Lord would have found another way to bring Mark and Linda together and closer to Him if I hadn't responded, but I was glad that I listened to the Spirit's prompting. This whole scenario reminds me of the movie, *It's a Wonderful Life,* which illustrated that the life of just one person can make a difference in many other lives.

The Lord told many parables about seeds and how they grow to produce fruit. One parable is of seeds growing without our help. We plant and He makes the seed sprout and grow within their hearts and souls. We notice the growth and are sometimes amazed at the results.

Let's look at the parable of the seed growing without our knowledge.

Mark 4: 26-32

[26] And He was saying, "The kingdom of God is like a man who casts seed upon the soil; [27] and he goes to bed at night and gets up by day, and the seed sprouts and grows—how, he himself does not know. [28] The soil produces crops by itself; first the blade, then the head, then the mature grain in the head. [29] But when the crop permits, he immediately puts in the sickle, because the harvest has come."

The smallest of seeds has the potential to make a significant difference in a life. Think about this. How did two small boys in Poland and Argentina become

Pope? How did Mother Theresa end up in Calcutta? I am sure many people and events were involved in planting and encouraging them along the way.

When we think about the Lord working within, we sometimes only think of others and not ourselves. From the time a seed was planted within us, the Lord and the Spirit have continued to help us increase our faith, understanding and desire to be with God forever in heaven. God is working within us at this very moment as we ponder this statement,-and through His grace we will continue to grow spiritually into the person He wants us to be.

Matthew: 13: 30-32

[30] And He said, "How shall we picture the kingdom of God, or by what parable shall we present it? [31] *It is* like a mustard seed, which, when sown upon the soil, though it is smaller than all the seeds that are upon the soil, [32] yet when it is sown, it grows up and becomes larger than all the garden plants and forms large branches; so that the birds of the air can nest under its shade."

Many of you have Christian friends who join you on vacations or doing other activities. You may have known them for 20, 30, 40 or 50 years and yet have never shared your spiritual beliefs.

When we sponsored our friends to a Cursillo three day weekend, it brought our 40 year friendship to a new level. We now enjoy a much deeper relationship with these friends. We are connected spiritually and we discuss faith openly. We share how the Lord is working in our lives and the lives of our families. We also have discussions on different books that are helping us grow in our knowledge of God.

All of us have long time friends, friends for a reason and friends for a season, but how many of them are also spiritual friends who help us grow in our faith? Think about it. How can you become a spiritual friend to them?

If you are one with Christ, the Lord will use you to provide encouragement for others. Respond to His prompting. The closer we come to knowing God, the more opportunities he will provide to spread the good news. When Christ sends someone to you, all He asks is for you to listen to his call and respond.

1 Corinthians 13:13

And now these three remain: faith, hope and love. But the greatest of these is love.

It was once said that the only thing that keeps the world from being what God intended is a lack of love and generosity. If you are one with Christ you exhibit both love and generosity and are a blessing to the world.

Questions for self-reflection or group discussion:

Who did God send into your life, that had an impact on your faith?

_____

_____

Is there someone with whom you would like to have a spiritual connection?

_____

How can you develop a deeper spiritual relationship with those you know?

_____

_____

Do you recall someone saying you were an angel? It may have been for doing a good deed, or saying the right thing at the right time. It could be you were responding to a prompting of the Spirit without knowing it.

_____

_____

Can you recall a time when you planted a seed and it brought a change in a person's life?

_____

_____

_____

How do we miss opportunities to plant seeds?

_____

_____

_____

Nothing can constrain the Spirit from completing God's will. Is the Spirit asking you to do something but you are not responding?

_____

_____

_____

_____

What are your experiences and thoughts for your story?

Chapter IX -- Inside the Red Circle

EXUDE GOD'S LOVE. God is the center of your life. You are one with Christ. You act in Him, for Him and with Him in all that you do. Every moment of your day from morning offering to bedtime prayer is offered to Him.

This is the circle we all strive to attain. It is elusive because of the dedication, discipline and the complete rendering of self that reaching this circle requires. We consider those who reach it to be saints. This is where God wants us to be. In almost every book of the Bible, and especially in the New Testament, Christ is asking us to be holy like our heavenly Father is holy. If we dedicate our lives to Christ, He will give us the strength and grace to become saints and complete the commission He has assigned to us.

Isaiah 41: 10

¹⁰ do not be afraid, for I am with you; do not be alarmed, for I am your God. I give you strength, truly I help you, truly I hold you firm with my saving right hand.

Once we become true disciples, He asks us to take the grace we have been given and act to bring others to Him. Our job is to encourage them to be one with Him.

Luke 10: 1-7 The Mission of the Seventy-two.

¹After this the Lord appointed seventy-two others and sent them two by two ahead of him to every town and place where he was about to go. ² He told them, "The harvest is plentiful, but the workers are few. Ask the Lord of the harvest, therefore, to send out workers into his harvest field. ³ Go! I am sending you out like lambs among wolves. ⁴ Do not take a purse or bag or sandals; and do not greet anyone on the road.⁵ When you enter a house, first say,'Peace to this house.' ⁶ If someone who promotes peace is there, your peace will rest on them; if not, it will return to you. ⁷ Stay there, eating and drinking whatever they give you, for the worker deserves his wages. Do not move around from house to house.

The 72 disciples are long gone from this earth. We are His disciples now.

In this parable many people miss the importance of the first line. Jesus said He sent them out ahead of Him. This means He followed them after they prepared men to hear and accept His message.

The same thing happens today when you ask someone to join you in your walk. The Lord is with you but he also stays with the seed you planted in their mind when you issued the invitation. He dwells within them and nurtures the seed long after they have given you their response.

Matthew 28: 18-20

[18] Jesus came up and spoke to them. He said, "All authority in heaven and on earth has been given to me.[19] Go, therefore, make disciples of all nations; baptize them in the name of the Father and of the Son and of the Holy Spirit."

In his book, *Life is Worth Living,* Bishop Fulton Sheen writes in the chapter entitled Three Degrees of Intimacy, the final paragraph.

> "There is nothing more that God can do to exhaust the intimacies of love. He has spoken; He has been seen; and He has been touched. To each and every person in the world He has given at least one of these intimacies. He is heard in His Scripture and by the invisible ear of the soul attentive to the whispering of His grace. He is seen by the eyes of faith in the poor and in His Body the Church, which has been growing in age and grace and wisdom through the centuries. The final intimacy of all is that of touch reserved only for the chosen few who enjoy a communion with Him that is almost an interpenetration of the Divine and the Human, an embrace of love

when He who is the Divine Host comes into the human heart as its Guest. It does not require much time to make us Saints. It only requires much love."

The key phrase in this is, "when the Divine Host comes into the human heart as its Guest." All we need do to become a saint is to invite Him into our hearts and listen to His voice. Soon we too could become saints.

What we have discussed here is being sent to bring others to Christ, knowing that He is with us. But what we are sharing with others is His love which He has bestowed upon us.

This love comes from His reassurance that His love is perfect and without reservation. He does not withhold it even when we fail to do His will. It was this love that gave us the encouragement early on to seek Him. When we express and share His love with others we unknowingly draw them to Him through us.

It was this love that Auxiliary Bishop Binzer was talking about when he said in his testimony that he recognized God's love in little moments, "moments when God enlightened me about how much God loved me."

Bishop Binzer commented that the moments were a result of the people on the team, who like the apostles were sharing the good news and the men on the weekend discussing what they understood in hearing the good news. Moments where God speaks to us or His presence is felt can happen any time someone does God's will. Perhaps it is not always profound, but He speaks to each of us through others and it is always uplifting.

During the Easter Vigil the priest takes the Easter candle and lights the candles of those near Him. The candle lighting spreads throughout the church. As more and more candles are lit the once small light grows into a glow which illuminates the entire church.

When we share the gospel, or use our gifts to spread the love of God with those we meet, our light takes root in them. Now others are touched by God's love which is uplifting for them and encourages them to share kindness to those they meet.

Each time God's love is shared in any form: a smile, a helping hand a special moment, a sharing of the gospel, a spontaneous gesture or a donation, it illuminates those we touch. They take the light we gave them and share it with others. Soon our neighborhood, family, church, workplace and world will be illuminated. It does not take long for God's love to spread. All it takes is us sharing God's love and gifts each and every day. At the end of the day we will never know how many candles were lit because of our actions in sharing the love of God.

How many will you light tomorrow, along with using the spontaneous opportunities God places before you?

The sharing of God's love is a gift, a gift from God to us, from us to others. It is when we listen to His voice and do His will with love that we become one with Him and His joy shines like a beacon from within.

Questions for self-reflection or group discussion:

Do you think it is possible to become a saint?

_____

_____

Do you think evangelization is really a condition for entry into the Kingdom?

_____

_____

_____

When we evangelize others, we evangelize ourselves. We reinforce God's love as we share our life with others and plant seeds. Do you feel you plant seeds?

_____

_____

How many spiritual friends do you have where you openly share your faith and grow closer to Christ together?

_____

_____

What are your experiences and thoughts for your story?

Our Continuous Conversion

The purpose of the circles illustration is to provide a bench mark so we can evaluate our faith life and determine where we might be in our relationship with God. The programs and actions listed are by no means an exhaustive list, but they help to show us how we can grow closer to God.

In our busy lives we seldom take the time to evaluate just where we are in our relationship with Christ. One of the things that often hinders us on our journey is complacency. At every level we can settle into complacency. It becomes easy to compare ourselves to others instead of focusing on reaching out to those the Lord puts in our path. We may also be reluctant to share our faith because we know that we still have a long way to go ourselves.

Why do we become complacent? How does it happen? In the **Dark Blue** circle we think we are just fine going to church on Sunday and doing a few acts of mercy. In the **Light Blue** circle we are spending time reading the Bible or going to Bible study. What more does God want? In the **Lavender** circle we may think, I made a retreat a while back, I really don't need to spend more extended time with Him. I feel comfortable where I am at.

It is not until we start to get into the **Gold** circle that we really desire to become one with God. He is now our main focus. As we respond to His call, He continues to challenge us to grow in faith, and as we grow in faith we come to recognize him in our actions, thoughts and in others.

You know where you are now. The question is, "Where do you want to be?" Once you answer that question, ask God where He wants you to be. At that point you and God can be on the same page. You should have a clear vision for your spiritual life. The Spirit will be your personal guide. You will become aware of the opportunities He provides and have the courage to move forward. Jesus told us, "Fear not for I am always with you. Do not be afraid."

In all of the personal stories mentioned on these pages, the seeds which were planted took years to mature and required much nurturing. I am blessed to be able to see some of the plantings grow. Sometimes we are not shown the fruits of our labor, but that does not mean that our efforts are in vain.

Did you ever hear someone comment that they had heard something a 100 times but it wasn't until the 101st time that it struck home? Perhaps a friend refers back to something you said years ago which started them thinking.

At other times in a spiritual discussion someone may even give you credit for something you said and you do not remember it. The Spirit revealed something to them in your discussion and you may not even have said it. You provided the opportunity and Christ planted the seed. There are many times we have planted seeds without knowing it.

The point is that you never really know the value of your words or deeds. Every effort you make for Christ has value. Do not miss out on leading someone to a closer relationship with Christ. Respond to His prompting.

There are a few reasons for sharing my story. One is to promote self-awareness of where each one of us is in our walk with Christ. Another is to encourage all who read it to continue to seek a personal relationship with Christ. The third reason is to help all who read the book to visualize how they can bring people they know, love and can influence to a closer relationship with Christ.

You may have found the book challenging you in a new way. If so, you may want to read it again in the future to measure your progress and at the same time allow Christ to once again reveal His plan for you. Perhaps you will be able to write your own story on how Christ has used you to bring others to Him.

Remember that it is through His gift of the Holy Spirit that we are able to know, share and understand the Father's love and will. It is our loving Father who brings people to Him, we are just His instruments.

The Holy Spirit provided this simple book with the circle illustrations to encourage all of us to bring a new spirituality to our world by living a Christ like life. He guided me, and He will guide you as He works to draw you toward Him.

Conclusion

To get to the **Red** center may seem impossible, but the prize is worth the effort. You have a lifetime to work towards getting there. Of course each of us does not know how long our lifetime is. We need to start today to plan on how to get from where we are now to where we want to be. At the end of each day we must review and be assured that we did all we could to be with Him. Today and each day we need to focus and act on a plan to see Him face to face.

We know that it will be God who judges us in truth. If we should run out of time, God in His mercy may give us extra credit for our dedication to His Son Jesus Christ and our sincerity in our efforts from this day forward. Today is the most important day.

May the Lord bless you and give you the courage, grace and wisdom to become a saint.

May the Holy Spirit guide you and bless you with peace, joy and grace on your journey with Christ.

May you accomplish your purpose while here on earth with the knowledge that you indeed will be with your heavenly Father for eternity.

Clarence Gilles

Made in the USA
San Bernardino, CA
28 July 2015